holiday Jar MIXES

Andra Roberts and Wilma Teal

BARBOUR
PUBLISHING

ISBN 1-59310-888-5

All Scripture quotations are taken from the King James Version of the Bible.

Cover image © Jim Celuch/Celuch Creative Imaging

Published by Barbour Publishing, Inc., P.O. Box 719, Uhrichsville, Ohio 44683
www.barbourbooks.com

Our mission is to publish and distribute inspirational products offering exceptional value and biblical encouragement to the masses.

Member of the
Evangelical Christian
Publishers Association

Printed in Canada.
5 4 3 2 1

CONTENTS

Until one feels the spirit of Christmas, there is no Christmas. All else is outward display—so much tinsel and decorations. For it isn't the holly, it isn't the snow. It isn't the tree nor the firelight's glow. It's the warmth that comes to the hearts of men when the Christmas spirit returns again.

UNKNOWN

These wintry jar mixes make the perfect gifts for the hard-to-buy-for people on your Christmas list. With bread mixes, soup mixes, cake mixes, and everything in between, you're guaranteed to find dozens of gift ideas so you can handle the holiday rush with ease.

Every good gift
and every perfect gift
is from above.

JAMES 1:17

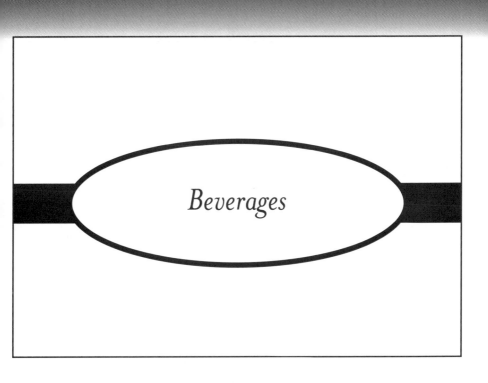

Chocolate Raspberry Smoothie Mix

2 cups instant raspberry drink mix
2 cups instant chocolate milk drink mix

In a medium bowl, combine ingredients. Spoon smoothie mix into a 1-quart glass jar or two 1-pint glass jars. Attach a recipe card with the following instructions.

Chocolate Raspberry Smoothies

1¾ cups milk

¼ cup Chocolate Raspberry
Smoothie Mix

In a large glass, place ¼ cup smoothie mix. Add milk. Stir well and enjoy!

Chocolate Raspberry Milkshakes

½ cup milk
¾ cup vanilla or chocolate ice cream

⅓ cup Chocolate Raspberry
Smoothie Mix

Place all ingredients in a blender or food processor. Process until smooth. Pour into a large glass and enjoy!

Cinnamon Vanilla Nut Cappuccino Mix

1 (8 ounce) jar instant coffee granules
2 (8 ounce) jars vanilla nut-flavored
   nondairy creamer

2 teaspoons ground cinnamon
1 cup powdered sugar
¼ teaspoon salt

In a large bowl, combine all ingredients. Spoon Cinnamon Vanilla Nut Cappuccino Mix into a 1-quart glass jar. Attach a recipe card with the following instructions.

Cinnamon Vanilla Nut Cappuccino

Place 2 tablespoons Cinnamon Vanilla Nut Cappuccino Mix into a mug. Add 6 to 8 ounces boiling water. Stir and enjoy!

GIFT IDEA: Place Cinnamon Vanilla Nut Cappuccino Mix in a basket with Cappuccino Brownie Mix.

French Vanilla Hot Cocoa Mix

2½ cups nonfat dry milk powder

1¼ cups powdered sugar

½ cup unsweetened cocoa powder

½ cup French vanilla–flavored nondairy creamer

In a large bowl, combine all ingredients. Spoon into a 1-quart glass jar. Attach a recipe card with the following instructions.

French Vanilla Hot Cocoa

Place ⅓ cup French Vanilla Hot Cocoa Mix into a mug. Add 6 to 8 ounces boiling water. Stir and enjoy!

Hot Spiced Tea Mix

⅓ cup instant tea with lemon
⅔ cup instant orange breakfast
    drink mix

1 cup sugar
½ teaspoon cloves
1 teaspoon cinnamon

In a medium bowl, combine all ingredients, stirring well to mix. Spoon Hot Spiced Tea Mix into a 1-pint glass jar. Attach a recipe card with the following instructions.

Hot Spiced Tea

Place 2 teaspoons Hot Spiced Tea Mix into a cup. Add 8 ounces boiling water. Stir and enjoy!

Merry Mocha Mix

2½ cups nonfat dry milk powder
1⅓ cups powdered sugar
⅓ cup unsweetened cocoa powder

½ cup chocolate-flavored nondairy
  creamer
¼ cup instant coffee granules

In a large bowl, combine all ingredients. Spoon Merry Mocha Mix into a 1-quart glass jar. Attach a recipe card with the following instructions.

Merry Mocha

Place ⅓ cup Merry Mocha Mix into a mug. Add 6 to 8 ounces boiling water. Stir and enjoy!

Minty Hot Cocoa Mix

2½ cups nonfat dry milk powder
1 cup powdered sugar
½ cup unsweetened cocoa powder

½ cup nondairy creamer
⅓ cup soft peppermint candies

Place all ingredients in an electric food processor, and process until mixture becomes a fine powder. Spoon Minty Hot Cocoa Mix into a 1-quart glass jar. Attach a recipe card with the following instructions.

Minty Hot Cocoa

Place ⅓ cup Minty Hot Cocoa Mix into a mug. Add 6 to 8 ounces boiling water. Stir well.

GIFT IDEA: Place Minty Hot Cocoa Mix in a basket with 2 mugs and peppermint sticks.

Malted Hot Cocoa Mix

2 cups nonfat dry milk powder
½ cup malted milk powder
½ cup unsweetened cocoa powder

1¼ cups powdered sugar
½ cup nondairy powdered creamer

In a medium bowl, combine all ingredients, mixing well. Spoon mix into a 1-pint glass jar. Attach a recipe card with the following instructions.

Malted Hot Cocoa

Place ⅓ cup Malted Hot Cocoa Mix into a mug. Add 6 to 8 ounces boiling water. Stir well and enjoy!

Spiced Chai Mix

¾ cup nonfat dry milk powder
¼ cup plus 2 tablespoons vanilla-
     flavored powdered nondairy
     coffee creamer
¼ cup plus 2 tablespoon unsweetened
     instant tea

⅓ cup powdered sugar
2½ teaspoons ground cinnamon
1 teaspoon ground cardamom
1 teaspoon ground cloves
½ teaspoon allspice

In a small bowl, combine all ingredients. Spoon Spiced Chai Mix into a 1-pint glass jar. Attach a recipe card with the following instructions.

Spiced Chai

Place 3 to 4 heaping teaspoons Spiced Chai Mix into a cup. Add 8 ounces boiling water. Stir and enjoy!

Vanilla Orange Smoothie Drink Mix

2 cups instant orange-flavored breakfast drink mix
2 cups vanilla-flavored milk drink mix

In a medium bowl, combine all ingredients. Spoon Vanilla Orange Smoothie Drink Mix into a 1-quart glass jar or two 1-pint glass jars. Attach a recipe card with the following instructions.

Vanilla Orange Smoothie

¼ cup Vanilla Orange Smoothie
    Drink Mix

1¾ cups milk

In a blender, combine all ingredients and process until smooth. Pour into a glass and enjoy!

Vanilla Orange Smoothie Milkshake

⅓ cup Vanilla Orange Smoothie
    Drink Mix

½ cup milk
¾ cup vanilla ice cream

In a blender, combine all ingredients and process until smooth. Pour into a glass and enjoy!

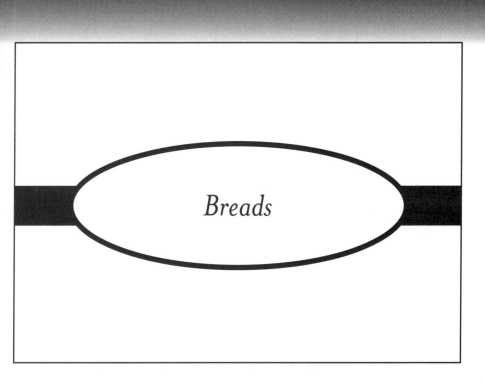

Breads

Cowboy Cornbread Mix

1 cup yellow or white cornmeal
1 cup all-purpose flour
3 tablespoons sugar

½ teaspoon salt
4 teaspoons baking powder
2 tablespoons dried, minced chives

Combine all ingredients thoroughly. Spoon cornbread mix into a, 1-pint wide-mouthed glass jar. Attach a recipe card with the following instructions.

Cowboy Cornbread

Cowboy Cornbread Mix   1 (8 ounce) container sour cream
2 eggs   ½ cup cooking oil

Preheat oven to 425 degrees. Grease an 8-inch square pan, 8-inch cast-iron skillet, or cast-iron cornbread mold. Place Cowboy Cornbread Mix in a large mixing bowl. Add eggs, sour cream, and oil. Beat with a spoon until smooth, about one minute. Do not overbeat. Bake for 20 to 25 minutes for pan or cast-iron skillet; 15 to 20 minutes for cornbread mold.

GIFT IDEA: This makes a great gift when placed in a basket, paired with Southwestern Soup Mix and bandana napkins.

Banana Nut Bread Mix

1 cup all-purpose flour
1 teaspoon baking soda
¼ teaspoon salt
¼ teaspoon nutmeg

¼ teaspoon cinnamon
½ cup whole wheat flour
½ cup sugar
½ cup chopped walnuts

In a medium bowl, combine all ingredients. Spoon Banana Nut Bread Mix into a 1-pint glass jar, tapping jar to settle ingredients. Attach a recipe card with the following instructions.

Banana Nut Bread

Banana Nut Bread Mix
½ cup butter, softened
2 eggs

3 large bananas, mashed
1 teaspoon vanilla

Preheat oven to 350 degrees. Grease and flour a 9x5x3-inch loaf pan. Place Banana Nut Bread Mix in a large bowl. Add butter, eggs, mashed bananas, and vanilla. Beat with an electric mixer until well combined. Pour batter into prepared pan. Bake for 50 to 60 minutes or until toothpick inserted near center comes out clean. Invert bread onto wire rack to cool.

Orange Cranberry Nut Bread Mix

¾ cup sugar
1 cup dried cranberries
3 cups pancake mix or baking mix

1 tablespoon dried, grated orange
    peel
½ cup chopped walnuts

Layer ingredients in order given in a 1-quart widemouthed jar. The ingredients must be packed very tightly. Attach a recipe card with the following instructions.

Orange Cranberry Nut Bread

Orange Cranberry Nut Bread Mix   1 egg, slightly beaten
1¼ cups orange juice

Preheat oven to 350 degrees. In a large bowl, combine orange juice and egg. Add Orange Cranberry Nut Bread Mix to the orange juice mixture, and beat with a wooden spoon until mixture is well combined. Pour bread dough into a greased 9x5x3-inch loaf pan. Bake for 55 to 60 minutes. Test with toothpick for doneness. Remove from pan and cool before slicing.

Grandma's Biscuit Mix

2 cups all-purpose flour
4 teaspoons baking powder

½ teaspoon plus 2 dashes salt
½ teaspoon cream of tartar

Sift above ingredients, and place in a 1-pint jar. Attach a recipe card with the following instructions.

Grandma's Biscuits

Grandma's Biscuit Mix
½ cup butter

⅔ cup milk
1 tablespoon mayonnaise

Place Grandma's Biscuit Mix in a bowl; cut in butter then make a well in the center of the ingredients. Combine milk and mayonnaise with mixture, and gently mix until all ingredients are combined. On floured surface, roll dough ½-inch thick. Cut with 2-inch biscuit cutter, and place close together on an ungreased cookie sheet. Bake at 450 degrees for 12 to 15 minutes. Serve warm with butter and honey—Yum!

GIFT IDEAS: Attach biscuit cutter with a ribbon to the jar mix, or give gift in a basket with biscuit mix, biscuit cutter, and honey or jam.

Cream and Sugar Tea Bread Mix

2½ cups all-purpose flour
1½ tablespoons baking powder
½ teaspoon baking soda

2 (3.4 ounce) packages instant
   vanilla pudding
1 cup sugar
½ cup finely chopped pecans

In a medium bowl, combine all ingredients. Spoon bread mix into a 1-quart glass jar. Attach a recipe card with the following instructions.

Cream and Sugar Tea Bread

3 ounces cream cheese, softened
½ cup butter, softened
2 eggs, slightly beaten

8 ounces sour cream
Cream and Sugar Tea Bread Mix

Preheat oven to 350 degrees. Grease and flour two 7½x3½x2-inch loaf pans. In a large mixing bowl, combine cream cheese and butter; cream until fluffy. Add eggs and sour cream, mixing until well blended. Stir in Cream and Sugar Tea Bread Mix and beat on low speed until combined. Pour batter into prepared pans. Bake for 40 to 45 minutes or until toothpick inserted near center comes out clean. Cool in pan 10 minutes before removing to wire rack.

GIFT IDEA: Place in small basket with Earl Grey Tea and teacup.

Cinnamon Raisin Quick Bread Mix

1½ cups all-purpose flour
½ teaspoon baking soda
¼ teaspoon baking powder
¼ teaspoon salt
1½ teaspoons ground cinnamon

½ cup packed brown sugar
¾ cup granulated sugar
1 cup raisins
¾ cup chopped pecans

In a medium bowl, combine flour, baking soda, baking powder, salt, and cinnamon. Place in bottom of 1-quart glass jar. Layer remaining ingredients in order given. Attach a recipe card with the following instructions.

Cinnamon Raisin Quick Bread

Cinnamon Raisin Quick Bread Mix
⅓ cup butter, softened
1 egg

½ cup milk
½ teaspoon vanilla

Preheat oven to 350 degrees. Grease and flour 9x5x3-inch loaf pan. Place Cinnamon Raisin Quick Bread Mix in a large bowl, stirring to combine. Add butter, egg, milk, and vanilla. Beat with an electric mixer until well blended. Pour batter into prepared pan. Bake for 55 to 60 minutes or until toothpick inserted near center comes out clean. Cool 10 minutes in pan before inverting onto a wire rack.

Lemon Poppy Seed Bread Mix

2½ cups all-purpose flour
3½ teaspoons baking powder
1 teaspoon salt
1 cup sugar

¼ cup poppy seeds
1½ tablespoons dried, grated
   lemon peel

Combine all ingredients, and pour into a 1-quart widemouthed glass jar. Attach
a recipe card with the following instructions.

Lemon Poppy Seed Bread

1¼ cups buttermilk
3 tablespoons vegetable oil
1 egg

1½ teaspoons lemon extract
Lemon Poppy Seed Bread Mix

Preheat oven to 350 degrees. In a large bowl, combine buttermilk, oil, egg, and lemon extract. Add Lemon Poppy Seed Bread Mix. Beat 30 seconds with a spoon. Pour into one 9x5x3-inch loaf pan or two 8½x4½x2½-inch loaf pans. Bake for 55 to 65 minutes or until toothpick inserted near center comes out clean. Cool 10 minutes in pan(s) before removing to wire rack. Cool completely, about 1 hour, before slicing. Wrap in plastic wrap, and store in refrigerator up to 1 week.

Pumpkin Spice Bread Mix

1 cup granulated sugar
1 cup packed brown sugar
3½ cups all-purpose flour
2 teaspoons baking soda

½ teaspoon baking powder
1 teaspoon salt
1 tablespoon pumpkin pie spice
1 cup chopped pecans

In a 1-quart widemouthed jar, layer ingredients in order given, combining flour, baking soda, baking powder, salt, and spice. Attach a recipe card with the following instructions.

Pumpkin Spice Bread

¾ cup vegetable oil
4 eggs
1 (15 ounce) can pumpkin

2 teaspoons vanilla
⅔ cup water
Pumpkin Spice Bread Mix

Preheat oven to 325 degrees. Grease and flour two 9x5x3-inch loaf pans. In a large mixing bowl, combine oil, eggs, pumpkin, and vanilla. Add Pumpkin Spice Bread Mix alternately with water. Spoon batter into prepared pans. Bake for 1 hour and 15 minutes or until toothpick inserted near center comes out clean. Let cool in pans for 10 minutes before turning out onto a wire rack.

Blueberry Muffin Mix

1¾ cups all-purpose flour
½ cup sugar

2 teaspoons baking powder
1 teaspoon dried, grated lemon peel

In a medium bowl, combine all ingredients. Spoon muffin mix into a 1-pint glass jar. Attach a recipe card with the following instructions.

Blueberry Muffins

Blueberry Muffin Mix
1 egg, slightly beaten
¾ cup milk

¼ cup vegetable oil
¾ cup fresh or frozen blueberries

Preheat oven to 400 degrees. Line muffin tin with paper baking cups. In a large bowl, empty Blueberry Muffin Mix. Add egg, milk, and oil, stirring with a spoon until combined. Fold in blueberries. Pour batter into baking cups until ⅔ full. Bake for 20 minutes or until lightly golden. Remove muffins from tin to a wire rack to cool slightly. Serve warm.

Cranberry Ginger Muffin Mix

1 cup sugar
2 cups all-purpose flour
1½ teaspoons baking powder
½ teaspoon baking soda

1 tablespoon finely chopped
  crystallized ginger
1 cup dried cranberries
¾ cup chopped walnuts

In a 1-quart widemouthed glass jar, layer ingredients in order given, combining flour, baking powder, baking soda, and ginger. Attach a recipe card with the following instructions.

Cranberry Ginger Muffins

Cranberry Ginger Muffin Mix
⅓ cup vegetable oil
½ cup milk

¼ cup orange juice
2 eggs, slightly beaten
½ tablespoon vanilla

Preheat oven to 350 degrees. Line muffin tin with paper baking cups. In a large bowl, empty Cranberry Ginger Muffin Mix, stirring to combine. Add oil, milk, juice, eggs, and vanilla. Stir until dry ingredients are just moistened. Spoon batter into prepared baking cups. Bake for 25 to 30 minutes or until toothpick inserted near center comes out clean.

Maple-Nut Breakfast Muffin Mix

1 cup whole wheat flour
1¼ cups all-purpose flour
2 teaspoons baking powder

½ teaspoon baking soda
¼ teaspoon salt
¼ cup finely chopped pecans

In a medium bowl, combine all ingredients. Spoon muffin mix into a 1-pint glass jar, tapping slightly to settle ingredients. Attach a recipe card with the following instructions.

Maple-Nut Breakfast Muffins

Maple-Nut Breakfast Muffin Mix
3 large eggs, slightly beaten
¼ cup honey
¼ cup maple syrup

⅔ cup vegetable oil
1 cup milk
1 teaspoon vanilla

Preheat oven to 375 degrees. Grease a 12-cup muffin tin, or line muffin tin with paper baking cups. In a large bowl, empty Maple-Nut Breakfast Muffin Mix. Make a well in the center and add remaining ingredients. Stir with spoon until just combined. Fill baking cups ⅔ full. Bake for 15 to 17 minutes or until lightly golden. Remove muffins from tin and cool on wire rack.

Sugar-Crusted Orange Muffin Mix

1¾ cups all-purpose flour
⅓ cup sugar
2 teaspoons baking powder

2 teaspoons dried, grated
   orange peel
¼ teaspoon cloves

In a medium bowl, combine all ingredients. Spoon muffin mix into a 1-pint glass jar, tapping slightly to settle if necessary. Attach a recipe card with the following instructions.

Sugar-Crusted Orange Muffins

Sugar-Crusted Orange Muffin Mix
¼ cup milk
½ cup orange juice

1 egg, slightly beaten
¼ cup vegetable oil
Additional sugar

Preheat oven to 400 degrees. Grease muffin tin, or line with paper baking cups. In a large bowl, empty Sugar-Crusted Orange Muffin Mix. Add milk, juice, egg, and vegetable oil. Stir with spoon until just combined. Fill baking cups ⅔ full. Sprinkle each muffin with a generous amount of additional sugar. Bake for 17 to 20 minutes or until golden brown.

Gingerbread Raisin Scone Mix

2¼ cups all-purpose flour
1 teaspoon baking powder
¼ teaspoon baking soda
1¼ teaspoons cinnamon
½ teaspoon ginger

¼ teaspoon allspice
¼ teaspoon ground nutmeg
⅛ teaspoon ground cloves
½ cup raisins

In a medium bowl, combine first 8 ingredients. Spoon flour mixture into a 1-pint widemouthed glass jar. Tap slightly to settle. Top with raisins. Attach a recipe card with the following instructions.

Gingerbread Raisin Scones

Gingerbread Raisin Scone Mix
½ cup butter

⅓ cup molasses
¾ cup whipping cream

Preheat oven to 425 degrees. Carefully remove raisins from Gingerbread Raisin Scone Mix. In a large mixing bowl, empty remaining contents of scone mix. Cut in butter with pastry blender until mixture is crumbly. Stir in raisins. Add molasses and whipping cream, stirring until just moistened. Turn dough out onto a lightly floured surface, and knead 4 to 5 times. Roll dough to ½-inch thickness on a lightly floured surface. Cut with a 2-inch biscuit cutter. Place scones on a lightly greased cookie sheet, and bake for 8 to 10 minutes. Serve warm with whipped cream.

GIFT IDEA: Tie a ribbon around the jar with recipe card and a 2-inch biscuit cutter.

Cakes

Apple Spice Cake Mix

¾ cup granulated sugar
1¼ cups packed brown sugar
1 cup dried apples, chopped
2 cups all-purpose flour
1 teaspoon baking soda

1 teaspoon baking powder
1½ teaspoons ground cinnamon
½ teaspoon ground nutmeg
¼ teaspoon cloves

In a 1-quart glass jar, layer ingredients in order given, combining flour, baking soda, baking powder, and spices. Attach a recipe card with the following instructions.

Apple Spice Cake

Apple Spice Cake Mix
1 cup butter, softened
2 large eggs

1 cup buttermilk
1½ teaspoons vanilla
Frosting or powdered sugar,
  optional

Preheat oven to 350 degrees. Grease and flour bundt pan or 9x13-inch cake pan. In a large bowl, empty contents of Apple Spice Cake Mix, stirring to combine. Add butter, eggs, buttermilk, and vanilla. Beat with a spoon until well blended. Pour batter into prepared pan. Bake for 45 to 55 minutes or until toothpick inserted near center comes out clean. For bundt cake, cool in pan 5 minutes before inverting onto a wire rack. Frost with frosting, or dust with powdered sugar, if desired.

Carrot Cake Mix

2½ cups all-purpose flour
¾ tablespoon baking powder
½ teaspoon baking soda
1 teaspoon ground ginger
½ teaspoon ground cloves
½ teaspoon ground allspice

½ teaspoon salt
¾ cup packed brown sugar
⅔ cup granulated sugar
¾ cup chopped walnuts
½ cup flaked coconut
½ cup raisins

Combine flour, baking powder, baking soda, spices, and salt. Place in bottom of a 1-quart glass jar. Layer remaining ingredients in order given. Attach a recipe card with the following instructions.

Carrot Cake

Carrot Cake Mix
3 large eggs
1 cup vegetable oil
¼ cup orange juice

1 tablespoon vanilla
Cream cheese frosting or powdered
   sugar, optional

Preheat oven to 350 degrees. Grease and flour bundt pan or 9x13-inch cake pan. In a large bowl, empty contents of Carrot Cake Mix, stirring to combine. Add eggs, oil, orange juice, and vanilla. Beat with a spoon until well blended. Pour into prepared pan. Bake for 40 to 50 minutes or until toothpick inserted near center comes out clean. For bundt pan, cool cake in pan for 5 minutes before inverting onto wire rack. Frost with cream cheese frosting, or dust with powdered sugar, if desired.

Chocolate Chip Cupcake Mix

3 cups all-purpose flour
2 cups granulated sugar
1 tablespoon baking powder

½ teaspoon salt
1 cup mini chocolate chips

In a large bowl, combine all ingredients. Spoon mixture into a 1-quart glass jar. Attach a recipe card with the following instructions.

Chocolate Chip Cupcakes

Chocolate Chip Cupcake Mix
1½ cups milk
½ cup butter, softened

2 teaspoons vanilla
2 eggs

Preheat oven to 375 degrees. Line muffin tin with paper baking cups. In a large mixing bowl, empty Chocolate Chip Cupcake Mix. Add milk, butter, and vanilla. Beat on low speed with an electric mixer until combined. Beat on high 2 minutes. Add eggs and beat 2 minutes more. Fill baking cups ½ full. Bake for 17 to 20 minutes or until toothpick inserted into a cupcake comes out clean. Remove cupcakes from pan and onto wire rack. Cool completely.

Chocolate Peanut Butter Cupcake Mix

2 cups all-purpose flour
1 teaspoon baking powder
2 teaspoons baking soda
½ cup packed brown sugar

1½ cups granulated sugar
¼ cup unsweetened cocoa powder
½ cup peanut butter chips

Combine flour, baking powder, and baking soda. Place in bottom of a 1-quart glass jar. Layer remaining ingredients in order given. Attach a recipe card with the following instructions.

Chocolate Peanut Butter Cupcakes

Chocolate Peanut Butter Cupcake
   Mix
½ cup creamy peanut butter
½ cup vegetable oil

1½ cups milk
2 eggs
Chocolate frosting, optional

Preheat oven to 350 degrees. Line muffin tin with paper baking cups. In a large mixing bowl, empty contents of Chocolate Peanut Butter Cupcake Mix, stirring to combine. Add peanut butter, oil, milk, and eggs. Beat on low speed with an electric mixer until well combined. Pour cupcake batter into baking cups, filling ⅔ full. Bake for 17 to 20 minutes or until toothpick inserted into a cupcake comes out clean. Remove cupcakes to wire rack and cool. Frost with chocolate frosting, if desired.

Coconut Cream Cake Mix

2 cups granulated sugar
1⅓ cups flaked coconut
2½ cups all-purpose flour

1 teaspoon baking powder
½ teaspoon baking soda

In a 1-quart glass jar, layer ingredients in order given, combining flour, baking powder, and baking soda. Attach a recipe card with following instructions.

Coconut Cream Cake

Coconut Cream Cake Mix
1⅓ cups milk
½ cup butter, softened
1 teaspoon vanilla

½ teaspoon almond extract
4 egg whites
Sweetened whipped cream
Additional flaked coconut, optional

Preheat oven to 350 degrees. Grease and flour two 9-inch round cake pans. In a large mixing bowl, empty contents of Coconut Cream Cake Mix, stirring to combine. Add milk, butter, vanilla, and almond extract. Beat on low with an electric mixer 30 seconds, scraping sides of bowl. Beat on medium to high speed 2 minutes. Add egg whites and beat 2 minutes more. Pour batter into prepared pans. Bake for 30 to 35 minutes or until toothpick inserted near center comes out clean. Cool in pans for 10 minutes before inverting to wire racks. Cool completely. Frost between layers, sides, and top with sweetened whipped cream. Sprinkle with additional coconut, if desired.

Double Chocolate Chip Cake Mix

(for the chocolate lover in your life)

2 cups sugar
¾ cup unsweetened cocoa powder
2¼ cups all-purpose flour

1 teaspoon baking soda
1 teaspoon salt
1½ cups semisweet chocolate chips

In a 1-quart widemouthed glass jar, layer ingredients in order given, combining flour, baking soda, and salt. Attach a recipe card with the following instructions.

Double Chocolate Chip Cake

1¼ cups butter, softened
2 teaspoons vanilla
5 eggs

Double Chocolate Chip Cake Mix
1 cup buttermilk
Favorite chocolate frosting

Preheat oven to 350 degrees. Grease and flour three 9-inch round cake pans. Carefully remove chocolate chips from Double Chocolate Chip Mix. Empty remaining contents of cake mix into a medium bowl, stirring to combine. In a large mixing bowl, cream butter until fluffy. Add vanilla and eggs; beat well. Add cake mix to creamed mixture alternately with buttermilk. Stir in chocolate chips. Pour batter into prepared pans, and bake for 30 to 35 minutes. Cool 10 minutes in pans before inverting to wire rack. Cool completely. Frost between layers, top, and sides.

Gingerbread Bundt Cake Mix

1 cup sugar
2 cups all-purpose flour
1 cup whole wheat flour
2 teaspoons baking soda

2 teaspoons ground ginger
2 teaspoons ground cinnamon
1 teaspoon allspice
½ teaspoon cloves

In a large bowl, combine all ingredients. Spoon mixture into a 1-quart glass jar. Attach a recipe card with the following instructions.

Gingerbread Bundt Cake

1 cup molasses
1 cup butter, melted and cooled
3 ounces cream cheese, softened
3 eggs

Gingerbread Bundt Cake Mix
1¼ cups boiling water
Powdered sugar, optional

Preheat oven to 350 degrees. Grease and flour a bundt pan. In a large mixing bowl, combine molasses, butter, cream cheese, and eggs. Beat with an electric mixer about 1 minute or until smooth. Add Gingerbread Bundt Cake Mix to the egg mixture alternately with the boiling water, beating on low speed until smooth. Pour batter into prepared pan. Bake for 40 to 50 minutes or until toothpick inserted near center comes out clean. Cool in pan on a wire rack 15 minutes before inverting cake onto wire rack to cool completely. Place cake on serving plate, and dust with powdered sugar, if desired.

Holiday Spice Cake Mix

2½ cups all-purpose flour
1¼ teaspoons baking powder
1¼ teaspoons baking soda
1¼ teaspoons cinnamon
¼ teaspoon cloves

½ teaspoon allspice
½ teaspoon ginger
1¼ cups sugar
½ cup packed brown sugar

In a medium bowl, combine all ingredients. Place mix in a 1-quart glass jar. Attach a recipe card with the following instructions.

Holiday Spice Cake

Holiday Spice Cake Mix
½ cup butter, softened
⅓ cup shortening
1¼ cups buttermilk

1 teaspoon vanilla
3 eggs
Cream cheese frosting, optional

Preheat oven to 350 degrees. Grease and flour two 9-inch round cake pans. In a large mixing bowl, empty Holiday Spice Cake Mix. Add butter, shortening, buttermilk, and vanilla. Beat with an electric mixer on low speed until combined. Beat 2 minutes on high speed. Add eggs and beat 2 minutes more. Pour batter into prepared pans. Bake for 30 to 35 minutes or until toothpick inserted near center comes out clean. Invert cakes onto wire rack and cool. Frost with cream cheese frosting, if desired.

Snowy Day Funnel Cake Mix

2 cups all-purpose flour
3 tablespoons sugar
¼ teaspoon salt

1 teaspoon baking powder
1½ teaspoons baking soda

In a medium bowl, combine all ingredients. Spoon mixture into a 1-pint glass jar, tapping jar to settle if necessary. Attach a recipe card with the following instructions.

Snowy Day Funnel Cakes

1 egg
¾ cup milk
Snowy Day Funnel Cake Mix

Oil for frying
Powdered sugar, optional

In a medium bowl, combine egg and milk; beat well. Add Snowy Day Funnel Cake Mix, and beat with a spoon or whisk until mixture is smooth. In a 10-inch skillet, pour oil to depth of 2 inches. Heat until hot, but not smoking. Pour batter into a funnel, holding finger over bottom hole. Hold funnel over skillet; removing finger, move funnel making circular designs to about 2 inches from side of skillet. When edges are brown, turn cake over and brown. Remove to paper towels. To serve, sprinkle with powdered sugar, or top with chocolate sauce or any fruit pie filling.

Sunshine Cake Mix

3 cups all-purpose flour
½ tablespoon baking powder
¾ teaspoon baking soda
2 cups sugar

2 teaspoons dried, grated
   orange peel
1 teaspoon dried, grated lemon
   peel

In a large bowl, combine all ingredients. Spoon into a 1-quart glass jar. Attach a recipe card with the following instructions.

Sunshine Cake

Sunshine Cake Mix
1 cup milk
½ cup orange juice
½ cup butter, softened
1 teaspoon vanilla

½ teaspoon orange extract
2 eggs
Cream cheese frosting or
    powdered sugar, optional

Preheat oven to 350 degrees. Grease and flour a 9x13x2-inch baking pan. In a large mixing bowl, empty Sunshine Cake Mix. Add milk, orange juice, butter, vanilla, orange extract, and eggs. Beat with an electric mixer until well blended. Pour cake batter into prepared pan. Bake for 30 to 40 minutes or until toothpick inserted near center comes out clean. Cool in pan on wire rack. Frost with cream cheese frosting, or dust with powdered sugar, if desired.

White Chocolate Holiday Fruitcake Mix

½ cup packed brown sugar
1⅓ cups all-purpose flour
2 teaspoons baking powder
¼ teaspoon salt
6 ounces white chocolate baking bar,
    chopped

½ cup chopped cashews
⅔ cup shredded coconut
⅓ cup candied orange peel, diced
½ cup macadamia nuts, chopped
¼ cup dried cranberries

In a 1-quart widemouthed jar, layer ingredients in order given, combining flour, baking powder, and salt. Attach a recipe card with the following instructions.

White Chocolate Holiday Fruitcake

White Chocolate Holiday
Fruitcake Mix

¼ cup butter, softened
3 large eggs

Preheat oven to 300 degrees. Grease a 9x5x3-inch loaf pan; line with waxed paper. Grease and flour waxed paper. Carefully remove white chocolate, nuts, orange peel, cranberries, and coconut from White Chocolate Holiday Fruitcake Mix. In a large mixing bowl, beat butter until fluffy. Add eggs and beat well. Add remaining contents of fruitcake mix in jar, beating on low speed until well blended. Fold in white chocolate, nuts, and fruit. Batter will be very thick and chunky. Spoon batter into prepared pan. Bake for 1 hour and 15 minutes. Run a sharp knife around edge of pan to loosen fruitcake; cool in pan on wire rack for 30 minutes. Invert to a wire rack and cool completely.

Cookies, Brownies & Bars

Butter Mint Sugar Cookie Mix

1 cup sugar
1 cup soft butter mint candies,
    crushed

2½ cups all-purpose flour
2 teaspoons baking powder
½ teaspoon salt

Combine flour, baking powder, and salt. Set aside. In a 1-quart glass jar, lightly layer ingredients in order given, ending with the flour mixture. Attach a recipe card with the following instructions.

Butter Mint Sugar Cookies

1 cup butter, softened
2 large eggs
1 teaspoon vanilla
½ teaspoon butter flavoring

1 tablespoon milk
Butter Mint Sugar Cookie Mix
¼ cup sugar

Preheat oven to 350 degrees. In a large mixing bowl, beat butter until fluffy. Add eggs, vanilla, and butter flavoring, beating until blended. Stir in milk. Add Butter Mint Sugar Cookie Mix, beating well. Cover and chill dough for an hour. Shape dough into 1-inch balls. Roll balls in ¼ cup sugar. Place balls 2 inches apart on an ungreased cookie sheet. Bake for 8 to 10 minutes or until barely golden. Cool 2 minutes on cookie sheet before removing to a wire rack.

Chocolate Chip Cookie Mix

¾ cup granulated sugar
½ cup packed brown sugar
1¾ cups all-purpose flour

¾ teaspoon baking soda
½ teaspoon salt
1½ cups semisweet chocolate chips

In a 1-quart glass jar, layer ingredients in order given, combining flour, baking soda, and salt. Attach a recipe card with the following instructions.

Chocolate Chip Cookies

Chocolate Chip Cookie Mix
¾ cup shortening
2 tablespoons milk

½ tablespoon vanilla
½ teaspoon butter flavoring
1 egg

Preheat oven to 350 degrees. In a large mixing bowl, empty Chocolate Chip Cookie Mix, stirring to combine. Add shortening, milk, vanilla, butter flavoring, and egg. Beat with a spoon or electric mixer until well blended. Drop by rounded tablespoonfuls 2 inches apart onto an ungreased cookie sheet. Bake for 11 to 13 minutes or until light brown. Cool 1 minute on cookie sheet before removing to a wire rack.

Chunky Peanut Butter Chocolate Chip Cookie Mix

¼ cup granulated sugar
½ cup chopped salted peanuts
¾ cup packed brown sugar
1¾ cups all-purpose flour

¾ teaspoon baking soda
½ teaspoon salt
½ cup semisweet chocolate chunks
½ cup milk chocolate chips

In a 1-quart glass jar, layer ingredients in order given, combining flour, baking soda, and salt. Attach a recipe card with the following instructions.

Chunky Peanut Butter Chocolate Chip Cookies

Chunky Peanut Butter Chocolate
    Chip Cookie Mix
¾ cup chunky peanut butter

½ cup butter, softened
1 egg
1 tablespoon vanilla

Preheat oven to 375 degrees. Carefully remove milk chocolate chips and semisweet chocolate chunks from Chunky Peanut Butter Chocolate Chip Cookie Mix; set aside. In a large mixing bowl, empty remaining contents of cookie mix, stirring well to combine. Add peanut butter, butter, egg, and vanilla. Beat with an electric mixer until well blended. Add chocolate chips and chunks, stirring to combine. Drop by rounded tablespoonfuls 2 inches apart onto an ungreased cookie sheet. Bake for 10 to 12 minutes or until lightly browned. Cool 2 minutes on cookie sheet before removing to a wire rack.

Loaded Oatmeal Raisin Cookie Mix

1 cup all-purpose flour
1 teaspoon baking soda
1 teaspoon ground cinnamon
½ teaspoon ground nutmeg
½ teaspoon ground cloves
½ teaspoon salt

¾ cup packed brown sugar
½ cup granulated sugar
½ cup raisins
1 cup quick-cooking oats
½ cup sliced almonds
½ cup butterscotch chips

In a bowl, combine the first six ingredients. Pour flour mixture into a 1-quart glass jar, and continue layering in order given. Attach a recipe card with the following instructions.

Loaded Oatmeal Raisin Cookies

¾ cup butter, softened
1 egg

1 teaspoon vanilla
Loaded Oatmeal Raisin Cookie
Mix

Preheat oven to 350 degrees. In a mixing bowl, cream butter. Beat in egg and vanilla. Add Loaded Oatmeal Raisin Cookie Mix and mix well. Drop by rounded teaspoonfuls 2 inches apart onto a greased cookie sheet. Bake for 9 to 11 minutes or until golden brown. Cool 2 minutes on cookie sheet before removing to a wire rack.

Molasses Cookie Mix

¼ cup granulated sugar
¾ cup packed brown sugar
2¼ cups all-purpose flour mixed with
    2 teaspoons baking soda

1¼ teaspoons cinnamon
1 teaspoon ground ginger
½ teaspoon ground cloves
¼ teaspoon salt

Layer ingredients in a 1-quart glass jar in order given. Attach a recipe card with the following instructions.

Molasses Cookies

¾ cup shortening
¼ cup molasses
1 egg

Molasses Cookie Mix
3 to 4 tablespoons granulated sugar

Preheat oven to 325 degrees. In a mixing bowl, cream shortening. Add molasses and egg, beating until well combined. In a large bowl, empty Molasses Cookie Mix, stirring to combine; add to creamed mixture. Mix until well combined. Shape dough into 1½-inch balls. Roll dough in granulated sugar, and place 2 inches apart on an ungreased cookie sheet. Bake for 12 to 15 minutes or just until set. Immediately remove cookies to a wire rack.

Pecan Tea Cookie Mix

½ cup granulated sugar
¾ cup packed brown sugar
1¾ cups all-purpose flour

¾ teaspoon baking soda
¾ teaspoon cinnamon
1 cup chopped pecans

In a 1-quart glass jar, layer ingredients in order given, combining flour, baking soda, and cinnamon. Attach a recipe card with the following instructions.

Pecan Tea Cookies

Pecan Tea Cookie Mix
½ cup butter, softened

½ teaspoon vanilla
1 egg

Preheat oven to 350 degrees. In a large mixing bowl, empty Pecan Tea Cookie Mix, stirring to combine. Add butter, vanilla, and egg. Beat with a spoon or electric mixer until well blended. Shape dough into 1¼-inch balls. Place 2 inches apart on an ungreased cookie sheet. Bake for 10 to 12 minutes or until edges are lightly browned. Remove to a wire rack.

GIFT IDEA: Place Pecan Tea Cookie Mix in a gift basket along with a pretty teacup and some specialty teas.

Pecan-Toffee Shortbread Mix

¼ cup pecan pieces
½ cup packed brown sugar
½ cup toffee bits

2¼ cups all-purpose flour
⅛ teaspoon salt

Combine flour and salt; set aside. In a 1-quart glass jar, layer ingredients in order given, ending with the flour mixture. Attach a recipe card with the following instructions.

Pecan-Toffee Shortbread

Pecan-Toffee Shortbread Mix   1 teaspoon vanilla
1 cup butter, softened

Preheat oven to 275 degrees. In a medium bowl, empty Pecan-Toffee Shortbread Mix, stirring to combine; set aside. In a large mixing bowl, cream butter until fluffy. Add vanilla and stir. Add shortbread mix, beating until well blended. Roll dough out to ½-inch thickness, and cut into desired shapes. Place dough 2 inches apart on an ungreased cookie sheet. Bake for 45 to 50 minutes. Cool 2 minutes on cookie sheet before removing to a wire rack.

Triple Chocolate Chunk Cookie Mix

½ cup granulated sugar
¾ cup packed brown sugar
1¾ cups all-purpose flour
1 teaspoon baking soda
½ teaspoon salt

⅓ cup unsweetened cocoa powder
4 ounces white chocolate chunks
½ cup milk chocolate chips
⅓ cup semisweet chocolate chips

In a 1-quart glass jar, layer ingredients in order given, combining flour, baking soda, and salt. Attach a recipe card with the following instructions.

Triple Chocolate Chunk Cookies

Triple Chocolate Chunk Cookie Mix
1 cup butter, softened

1 teaspoon vanilla
2 eggs

Preheat oven to 325 degrees. Carefully remove semisweet chocolate chips, milk chocolate chips, and white chocolate chunks from Triple Chocolate Chunk Cookie Mix; set aside. In a mixing bowl, beat butter, vanilla, and eggs until creamy. In a large bowl, empty remaining contents of cookie mix, stirring to combine; add to creamed mixture until well blended. Stir in chocolate chips and white chocolate chunks. Drop by rounded tablespoonfuls onto an ungreased cookie sheet. Bake for 11 to 13 minutes or until cookies are set and appear dry. Cool 1 minute on cookie sheet before removing to a wire rack.

Tropical Jewel Cookie Mix

1¾ cups all-purpose flour
1 teaspoon baking powder
½ teaspoon baking soda
½ teaspoon salt
½ teaspoon allspice
¾ cup packed brown sugar

⅓ cup granulated sugar
½ cup semisweet chocolate chips
½ cup white baking chips
½ cup flaked coconut
⅓ cup dried pineapple, chopped
⅓ cup macadamia nuts, chopped

Combine flour, baking powder, baking soda, salt, and allspice. Place in bottom of a 1-quart glass jar. Layer remaining ingredients in order given. Attach a recipe card with the following instructions.

Tropical Jewel Cookies

Tropical Jewel Cookie Mix
½ cup mashed ripe banana
1 egg

½ cup butter, softened
1 teaspoon vanilla

Preheat oven to 375 degrees. In a large bowl, empty Tropical Jewel Cookie Mix, stirring to combine. Add mashed banana, egg, butter, and vanilla. Beat with a spoon until well blended. Drop by rounded tablespoonfuls 2 inches apart onto an ungreased cookie sheet. Bake for 10 to 12 minutes or until lightly browned. Cool 2 minutes on cookie sheet before removing to a wire rack.

White Chocolate Cranberry Cookie Mix

½ cup packed brown sugar
½ cup granulated sugar
1 cup flour
1 teaspoon baking powder
¼ teaspoon baking soda

¼ teaspoon salt
1 cup old-fashioned oats
4 ounces white chocolate baking
    bar, chopped
½ cup dried cranberries

In a 1-quart widemouthed jar, layer ingredients in order given, combining flour, baking powder, baking soda, and salt. Attach a recipe card with the following instructions.

White Chocolate Cranberry Cookies

White Chocolate Cranberry
   Cookie Mix
⅔ cup butter, softened

1 large egg
½ tablespoon vanilla

Preheat oven to 375 degrees. Carefully remove cranberries and white chocolate from White Chocolate Cranberry Cookie Mix; set aside. In a large mixing bowl, empty remaining contents of cookie mix. Add butter, egg, and vanilla. Beat with an electric mixer until well blended. Stir in white chocolate and cranberries. Drop by rounded tablespoonfuls 2 inches apart onto an ungreased cookie sheet. Bake for 10 minutes or until lightly browned. Cool 2 minutes on cookie sheet before removing to a wire rack.

Chocolate Mint Brownie Mix

2 cups granulated sugar
¾ cup unsweetened cocoa powder
1 cup all-purpose flour

¾ teaspoon salt
1 teaspoon baking powder
1 cup chopped chocolate mint wafers

In a 1-quart glass jar, layer ingredients in order given, combining flour, salt, and baking powder. Attach a recipe card with the following instructions.

Chocolate Mint Brownies

Chocolate Mint Brownie Mix
1 cup butter, softened

3 eggs, slightly beaten
1½ teaspoons vanilla

Preheat oven to 350 degrees. Grease and flour a 9x13x2-inch baking pan. In a large mixing bowl, empty contents of Chocolate Mint Brownie Mix, stirring to combine. Add butter, eggs, and vanilla. Beat with a spoon until well blended. Spread batter into prepared pan. Bake for 35 to 40 minutes or until toothpick inserted near center comes out clean. Cool in pan on a wire rack. Cut into squares.

Rich Chocolate Fudge Brownie Mix

2 cups all-purpose flour
1 teaspoon baking soda
1 cup packed brown sugar

⅓ cup unsweetened cocoa powder
1 cup granulated sugar
1½ cups semisweet chocolate chips

Combine flour and baking soda. Place in bottom of a 1-quart glass jar. Layer remaining ingredients in order given. Attach a recipe card with the following instructions.

Rich Chocolate Fudge Brownies

Rich Chocolate Fudge Brownie Mix
1 cup butter, softened
2 eggs

1 teaspoon vanilla
1½ cups buttermilk

Preheat oven to 400 degrees. Grease and flour a 9x13x2-inch baking pan. In a large mixing bowl, empty contents of Rich Chocolate Fudge Brownie Mix, stirring well to combine. Add butter, eggs, vanilla, and buttermilk. Beat until well blended. Spread batter into prepared pan. Bake for 35 to 40 minutes or until toothpick inserted near center comes out clean.

Chocolate Chip Oat Bar Mix

1½ cups rolled oats
½ cup raisins
½ cup pine nuts

½ cup chopped, salted or
    honey-roasted peanuts
¾ cup semisweet chocolate chips

In a 1-quart glass jar, layer ingredients in order given. Attach a recipe card with the following instructions.

Chocolate Chip Oat Bars

Chocolate Chip Oat Bar Mix
⅔ cup sweetened, condensed milk

¼ cup butter, melted

Preheat oven to 325 degrees. Line a 9-inch square baking pan with foil, and butter foil. In a large bowl, empty Chocolate Chip Oat Bar Mix, stirring to combine. Add sweetened, condensed milk and mix well. Stir in melted butter until well blended. Spread oat mixture into prepared pan. Bake for 25 to 30 minutes or until top is light brown. Cool slightly in pan. Lift bars by foil and place on cutting board. Cut into bars.

Maple Almond Bar Mix

2½ cups all-purpose flour
¾ teaspoon baking soda
¼ teaspoon salt

1 cup packed brown sugar
¼ cup granulated sugar
¾ cup sliced almonds

Combine flour, baking soda, and salt. Place in bottom of a 1-quart glass jar. Layer remaining ingredients in order given. Attach a recipe card with the following instructions.

Maple Almond Bars

Maple Almond Bar Mix
½ cup butter, softened
½ cup maple syrup

2 eggs
½ cup milk
¼ teaspoon maple flavoring

Preheat oven to 350 degrees. Grease a 9x13x2-inch cake pan. In a large mixing bowl, empty Maple Almond Bar Mix, stirring to combine. Add butter, syrup, eggs, milk, and maple flavoring. Beat on medium speed with an electric mixer until blended. Spread batter evenly in prepared pan. Bake for 40 to 45 minutes or until toothpick inserted in center comes out clean. Place pan on a wire rack to cool. Cut into bars.

Spiced Applesauce Bar Mix

2 cups all-purpose flour
¾ teaspoon baking soda
1 teaspoon ground cinnamon
¼ teaspoon ground cloves

1 cup raisins
1 cup granulated sugar
1 cup chopped pecans

In a 1-quart glass jar, layer ingredients in order given, combining flour, baking soda, and spices. Attach a recipe card with the following instructions.

Spiced Applesauce Bars

Spiced Applesauce Bar Mix
½ cup butter, softened
2 eggs

1½ cups applesauce
1 teaspoon vanilla
Powdered sugar, optional

Preheat oven to 350 degrees. Grease and flour a 9x13x2-inch baking pan. In a large mixing bowl, empty Spiced Applesauce Bar Mix, stirring to combine. Add butter, eggs, applesauce, and vanilla. Beat with an electric mixer until well blended. Spread batter into prepared pan. Bake for 30 to 35 minutes or until toothpick inserted near center comes out clean. Cool completely in pan on a wire rack. Dust with powdered sugar, if desired. Cut into bars.

Dips & Soups

Holiday Spice Fruit Dip Mix

½ cup vanilla-flavored nondairy
  powdered creamer
¼ cup packed brown sugar
2 tablespoons ground cinnamon
1 tablespoon ground ginger

1 tablespoon ground allspice
1 tablespoon ground nutmeg
½ teaspoon salt
½ cup pecan pieces

In a medium bowl, combine all ingredients. Spoon into a 1-pint glass jar or two
½-pint glass jars. Attach a recipe card with the following instructions.

Holiday Spice Fruit Dip

4 ounces cream cheese, softened
¼ cup sour cream

2 tablespoons Holiday Spice Fruit
Dip Mix

In a small bowl, combine cream cheese and sour cream with Holiday Spice
Fruit Dip Mix, stirring until thoroughly blended. Serve with fruit and graham
crackers.

Onion-Dill Dip Mix

⅓ cup dill weed
⅓ cup dried parsley flakes
¼ cup dried, minced onion

1½ tablespoons Beau Monde
   seasoning
½ tablespoon garlic powder

In a small bowl, combine all ingredients, mixing well. Spoon Onion-Dill Dip Mix into a ½-pint glass jar. Attach a recipe card with the following instructions.

Onion-Dill Dip

2½ tablespoons Onion-Dill Dip Mix
8 ounces sour cream

1 cup mayonnaise

In a small bowl, combine Onion-Dill Dip Mix, sour cream, and mayonnaise. Cover and chill for at least 2 hours. Serve with raw vegetables and crackers.

Ranch Dip Mix

⅓ cup dried minced onion
3 tablespoons dried parsley flakes
3 teaspoons paprika
1½ tablespoons sugar

1½ tablespoons fresh ground pepper
1 tablespoon garlic powder
1½ tablespoons salt

In a small bowl, combine all ingredients. Spoon Ranch Dip Mix into a ½-pint jar. Attach a recipe card with the following instructions.

Ranch Dip

1 tablespoon Ranch Dip Mix   1 cup sour cream

In a small bowl, combine Ranch Dip Mix and sour cream. Chill for at least 1 hour before serving.

Southwestern Dip Mix

¼ cup dried, minced onion
4 tablespoons chili powder
3 tablespoons paprika
3 tablespoons ground cumin

2 tablespoons onion powder
1 tablespoon plus 1 teaspoon salt
3 tablespoons garlic powder
¼ teaspoon cayenne pepper

In a medium bowl, combine all ingredients. Spoon Southwestern Dip Mix into a
½-pint glass jar. Attach a recipe card with the following instructions.

Southwestern Dip

1 cup sour cream
4 ounces cream cheese, softened

1 tablespoon plus 1 teaspoon
  Southwestern Dip Mix

In a small bowl, combine all ingredients, beating until well blended. Chill for at least 1 hour before serving. Serve with vegetables or tortilla chips.

GIFT IDEA: Place Southwestern Dip Mix in small basket with package of chips. Tie with bandana.

Country Herb Lentil and Vegetable Soup Mix

3 tablespoons dried minced onion
2 tablespoons dried parsley
½ teaspoon oregano
½ teaspoon garlic pepper
2½ teaspoons salt
2 tablespoons beef bouillon granules

¼ cup barley
1 cup dried split peas
1 cup dried lentils
1 cup multicolored pasta
1 bay leaf

Combine minced onion, parsley, oregano, garlic pepper, salt, bouillon granules, and barley. Set aside. In a 1-quart widemouthed jar, layer peas, lentils, and pasta; top with spices and bay leaf. Seal. Attach a recipe card with the following instructions.

Country Herb Lentil and Vegetable Soup

Country Herb Lentil and Vegetable Soup Mix
3 quarts water
½ cup chopped celery
¼ cup chopped carrots
1 (1 pound) can of diced garlic herb tomatoes

Combine Country Herb Lentil and Vegetable Soup Mix with 3 quarts of water. Add celery, carrots, and tomatoes. Bring to boil, then simmer until vegetables are tender.

Creamy Tomato Bacon Soup Mix

2 tablespoon Italian seasoning
1 teaspoon salt
¼ teaspoon pepper
3 tablespoons all-purpose flour
⅓ cup plus 3 tablespoons powdered
  milk

¼ cup original coffee creamer
⅛ cup dried onion flakes
½ cup real bacon bits
1 bay leaf
¾ cup dried tomatoes

Combine Italian seasoning, salt, pepper, and flour; then add powdered milk, creamer, and onion flakes. In a 1-pint jar, layer milk mixture then bacon bits. Slip bay leaf in the front of the jar, making sure bacon bits hold half of it in place. Complete layering with dried tomatoes. Seal. Attach a recipe card with the following instructions.

Creamy Tomato Bacon Soup

2 cups water
Creamy Tomato Bacon Soup Mix

1 (28 ounce) can diced tomatoes

Bring 2 cups of water to a boil in a saucepan. Briskly stir in Creamy Tomato Bacon Soup Mix. After mixture is smooth, add canned tomatoes, cooking until mixture boils, stirring constantly. Makes approximately 6 servings.

GIFT IDEA: Place Creamy Tomato Bacon Soup Mix in a basket with crackers and cheese.

Hearty Bean Soup Mix

4 tablespoons dried yellow split peas
4 tablespoons dried green split peas
⅓ cup dried navy beans
⅓ cup kidney beans
⅓ cup great northern beans
⅓ cup pinto beans

2 tablespoons dried, minced onion
2½ teaspoons chicken bouillon granules
½ teaspoon cumin
¼ teaspoon garlic powder

In a 1-pint widemouthed glass jar, layer ingredients in order given. Attach a recipe card with the following instructions.

Hearty Bean Soup

8 cups water
Hearty Bean Soup Mix
1 cup chopped carrots

1 cup chopped celery
1 ham bone or 2 pounds ham hocks

In a 4-quart Dutch oven, heat water and Hearty Bean Soup Mix to boiling. Boil for 2 minutes, then remove from heat. Cover and let stand for 1 hour. Stir carrots and celery into bean mixture. Add ham bone and heat to boiling. Reduce heat; cover and simmer for about 2 hours or until beans are tender. Skim fat if necessary; remove ham bone, and remove ham from bone. Cut ham into desired-sized pieces, and add back into bean soup. Heat until hot.

GIFT IDEA: Pair Hearty Bean Soup Mix with Grandma's Biscuits or Cowboy Cornbread.

Italian Rice Soup Mix

1½ cups uncooked long grain
   brown rice
⅓ cup chicken bouillon granules

3 teaspoons dried parsley flakes
3 teaspoons Italian seasoning
¾ teaspoon freshly ground pepper

In a medium bowl, combine all ingredients. Spoon soup mix into a 1-pint glass jar. Attach a recipe card with the following instructions.

Italian Rice Soup

3 cups water   ⅔ cup Italian Rice Soup Mix
1 tablespoon butter

In medium saucepan, bring water, butter, and Italian Rice Soup Mix to a boil.
Reduce heat; cover and simmer for 30 to 35 minutes or until rice is tender.

Southwestern Soup Mix

1 package brown gravy mix
1½ tablespoons chili powder
½ tablespoon cayenne pepper
2 teaspoons dried oregano
2 teaspoons dried, minced chives

2 teaspoons cumin
2 tablespoons dried, minced onion
½ teaspoon garlic salt
12 tortilla chips, coarsely crushed
2 cups uncooked small penne pasta

Layer ingredients in a 1-quart jar in the order given. Attach a recipe card with
the following instructions.

Southwestern Soup

½ pound ground beef, browned
Southwestern Soup Mix
7 cups water

1 (15 ounce) can corn with red
   and green peppers
1 (16 ounce) can chopped tomatoes

In a Crock-Pot, combine browned beef, Southwestern Soup Mix, water, corn, and tomatoes. Simmer several hours or until pasta is fully cooked.

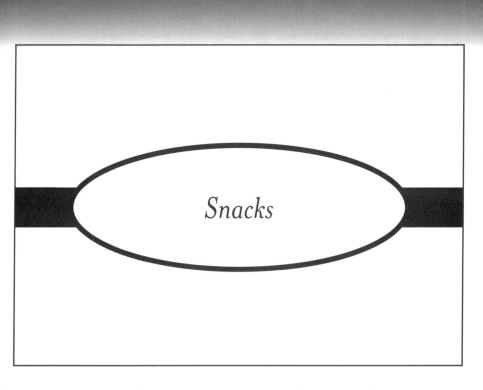

Snacks

Butterscotch and White Chocolate Cruncher

6 ounces butterscotch bits
6 ounces white chocolate chips
¼ cup crunchy peanut butter

8 cups cereal (corn flakes, crisp rice cereal, or toasted O's cereal)

In a double boiler, melt butterscotch and chocolate chips. Stir in peanut butter. Add cereal, and stir until well coated. Pour onto waxed paper. Let sit until cool (about 2 hours). Break apart, place in widemouthed jar, and seal. Should make two 1-quart jars or four 1-pint jars with a little left over to nibble on. Attach a card with holiday wishes.

Candied Trail Mix

¾ cup salted peanuts
½ cup semisweet chocolate chips
½ cup sunflower seeds
¾ cup candy-coated chocolate candies

½ cup honey-roasted peanuts
½ cup chocolate-covered raisins
½ cup salted cashews

In a 1-quart widemouthed jar, layer ingredients in order given. Attach a recipe card with the following instructions.

Candied Trail

Empty Candied Trail Mix into a serving dish, stirring to combine. Enjoy!

Chunky Rocky Road Mix

1 cup crushed pretzels
1 cup salted peanuts

½ cup marshmallows
1½ cups milk chocolate morsels

In a 1-quart widemouthed jar, layer the above ingredients in order given. Attach a recipe card with the following instructions.

Chunky Rocky Road

Remove chocolate morsels from mix and melt. Combine remainder of mix in bowl. Gently stir melted chocolate into other ingredients. Spread on waxed paper and cool. Break apart and enjoy!

Cranberry Christmas Snack Mix

1 cup yogurt-covered raisins
1 cup dried cranberries

1 cup small white chocolate-
covered pretzels
1 cup whole, salted almonds

In a 1-quart widemouthed glass jar, layer ingredients in order given. Attach a recipe card with the following instructions.

Cranberry Christmas Snack

Pour Cranberry Christmas Snack Mix into a serving bowl, stirring to combine. Enjoy!

Fruity Nut Snack Mix

¾ cup cashews
1 cup dried cranberries
¾ cup almonds

1 cup yogurt-covered raisins
½ cup pecan halves

In a 1-quart widemouthed jar, layer fruit and nuts in order given. Attach a recipe card with the following instructions.

Fruity Nut Snack

Empty contents of Fruity Nut Snack Mix into a serving bowl, stirring to combine. Enjoy!

Nuts about Bananas and Chocolate Snack Mix

1 cup semisweet chocolate chips
1 cup peanuts
1 cup dried banana chips

½ cup milk chocolate chips
½ cup peanut butter chips

In a 1-quart widemouthed jar, layer ingredients in order given. Attach a recipe card with the following instructions.

Nuts about Bananas and Chocolate Snack

Empty Nuts about Bananas and Chocolate Snack Mix into a serving bowl, stirring to combine. Enjoy!

Santa's Granola Munch Mix

2 cups uncooked old-fashioned oats
¼ cup sunflower seeds
⅓ cup wheat germ
⅓ cup crisp rice cereal
2 tablespoons packed brown sugar
3 tablespoons honey
3 tablespoons vegetable oil

2 tablespoons crunchy peanut butter
½ teaspoon vanilla
½ cup dried cranberries
½ cup dry-roasted peanuts
¾ cup red and green candy-coated
   chocolate pieces

Preheat oven to 325 degrees. Combine first 5 ingredients in a large bowl.
Combine honey, oil, peanut butter, and vanilla; pour over dry ingredients, tossing
to coat. Spread into a 15x10-inch baking pan. Bake for 20 minutes, stirring twice
during baking. Cool in pan. Stir in cranberries, peanuts, and chocolate candies.
Place Santa's Granola Munch Mix into a 1-quart glass jar or two 1-pint glass
jars. Attach gift card.

South of the Border Snack Mix

½ cup butter
1 tablespoon Worcestershire sauce
¼ teaspoon bottled hot pepper sauce
½ teaspoon onion salt
1 teaspoon chili powder
½ teaspoon ground cumin
½ teaspoon freshly ground pepper

¼ teaspoon garlic powder
1 cup salted peanuts
1 cup walnut halves
2 cups small pretzel twists
2 cups toasted O's cereal
2 cups square corn cereal

Preheat oven to 300 degrees. In a medium saucepan, combine butter, Worcestershire sauce, hot pepper sauce, and spices. Heat and stir until butter melts. In a large baking pan, mix nuts, pretzels, and cereals. Drizzle butter mixture over cereal mixture; toss to coat. Bake for 45 minutes, stirring every 15 minutes. Spread on foil to cool. Place South of the Border Snack Mix in two 1-quart jars or four 1-pint jars. Attach gift cards.

Spiced Honey Pecans

3 tablespoons butter
¼ cup granulated sugar
¼ cup honey
1 tablespoon orange juice

½ teaspoon cinnamon
¼ teaspoon cloves
¼ teaspoon salt
3 cups pecan halves

Preheat oven to 325 degrees. In a large saucepan, melt butter over medium heat. Add next 6 ingredients, stirring until sugar is dissolved. Add pecans, stirring to coat. Spread coated pecans onto a lightly greased 15x11-inch jelly roll pan. Bake for 15 minutes, stirring every 5 minutes. Cool completely. Break nuts apart. Place Spiced Honey Pecans into a 1-quart glass jar or two 1-pint glass jars. Attach gift cards.

Sugar and Spiced Almonds

¼ cup butter
¼ cup sugar

½ teaspoon cinnamon
2 cups whole salted almonds

Preheat oven to 300 degrees. In a medium saucepan, combine butter, sugar, and cinnamon. Cook over medium-low heat until sugar is dissolved. Add almonds, tossing to coat. Pour nuts into a greased, foil-lined baking pan. Bake for 20 to 25 minutes, stirring every 10 minutes. Cool in pan. Place Sugar and Spiced Almonds in a 1-pint glass jar. Attach gift card.

Spicy Popcorn Snack Mix

8 cups popped popcorn
4 cups pretzels
4 cups puffed corn snacks

¼ teaspoon chili powder
½ teaspoon garlic powder
¼ teaspoon onion powder

This will make four 1-quart jars. Best to use wide mouth.

Mix spices together and set aside. Layer each jar in the following order:

1 cup popcorn
1 cup pretzels

1 cup corn snack
1 cup popcorn

Divide the spice mixture into 4 equal parts, and sprinkle one part on top of each jar before sealing. Attach a recipe card with the following instructions.

Spicy Popcorn Snack

Spicy Popcorn Snack Mix   1 stick butter

Preheat oven to 325 degrees. Pour Spicy Popcorn Snack Mix in bowl, and stir gently to make sure spices are mixed well. Melt butter, and pour over popcorn mixture. Stir gently to make sure all is coated. Place on ungreased cookie sheet. Bake for 12 to 15 minutes. Stir halfway during baking time. Enjoy!

Sweet and Salty Cashews

¼ cup butter
¼ cup sugar
1 tablespoon honey

1 teaspoon salt
2 cups cashews

Preheat oven to 300 degrees. In a medium saucepan, combine butter, sugar, honey, and salt. Cook and stir until butter is melted and sugar is dissolved. Add cashews, stirring to coat. Pour mixture into a greased, foil-lined baking pan. Bake for 20 to 25 minutes, stirring every ten minutes. Cool in pan. Place Sweet and Salty Cashews in a 1-pint glass jar. Attach a gift card.

Specialty Diets—

BEVERAGES, BREADS, CAKES, COOKIES, BARS & BROWNIES

Spicy Hot Tea Mix
(sugar free, caffeine free)

¾ teaspoon ground cinnamon
¾ teaspoon ground cloves
¾ teaspoon ground allspice
1 cup sugar-free instant orange-flavored breakfast drink

½ cup unsweetened, caffeine-free instant tea
½ cup granulated sweetener (tested with Splenda)

In a medium bowl, combine all ingredients. Spoon Spicy Hot Tea Mix into a 1-pint glass jar. Attach a recipe card with the following instructions.

Spicy Hot Tea

Place 3 to 4 teaspoons of Spicy Hot Tea Mix into a cup. Add 1 cup boiling water; stir well. Enjoy!

Sugar-Free Hot Cocoa Mix

½ cup sugar-free vanilla-flavored
    creamer
¾ cup sugar-free chocolate milk
    drink mix

¼ cup nonfat dry milk powder
¼ cup granulated sweetener
3 tablespoons unsweetened cocoa
    powder

In a small bowl, combine all ingredients. Spoon Sugar-Free Hot Cocoa Mix into a 1-pint glass jar. Attach a recipe card with the following instructions.

Sugar-Free Hot Cocoa

Place 3 tablespoons Sugar-Free Hot Cocoa Mix in a cup. Add ¾ cup boiling water; stir well. Enjoy!

Banana Nut Bread Mix

(low fat, low sugar)

1½ cups whole wheat flour
1 teaspoon baking powder
½ teaspoon baking soda

⅓ cup raisins
⅓ cup chopped walnuts

In a 1-pint widemouthed glass jar, layer ingredients in order given, combining flour, baking powder, and baking soda. Attach a recipe card with the following instructions.

Banana Nut Bread

Banana Nut Bread Mix
1½ cups (3 medium) mashed ripe
    bananas
2 tablespoons honey

2½ tablespoons vegetable oil
1½ tablespoons lemon juice
1 teaspoon vanilla

Preheat oven to 350 degrees. Spray a 9x5x3-inch loaf pan with nonstick cooking spray. In a large bowl, empty contents of Banana Nut Bread Mix, stirring to combine. In a small bowl, combine remaining ingredients, and mix until well blended. Add banana mixture to the bread mix, stirring until well blended. Pour batter into prepared loaf pan. Bake for 35 to 40 minutes or until toothpick inserted near center comes out clean. Cool in pan for 10 minutes before inverting onto a wire rack.

Fat-Free Gingerbread Mix

1¼ cups packed brown sugar
2½ cups flour
1 teaspoon baking soda

2½ teaspoons cinnamon
1 teaspoon allspice
1 teaspoon ginger

Combine all ingredients thoroughly, and spoon into a 1-quart glass jar. Attach a recipe card with the following instructions.

Fat-Free Gingerbread

⅓ cup water
3 tablespoons honey
¼ cup applesauce

2 egg whites, slightly beaten
Fat-Free Gingerbread Mix

Preheat oven to 375 degrees. Spray an 8-inch square baking pan with cooking spray. In a large mixing bowl, combine water, honey, applesauce, and egg whites. Add Fat-Free Gingerbread Mix, and beat with an electric mixer until well combined. Pour into prepared pan. Bake for 40 to 45 minutes or until a toothpick inserted in center comes out clean.

Pumpkin Bread Mix

(low fat, low sugar)

1 cup whole wheat flour	¼ teaspoon salt
1 cup unbleached all-purpose flour	¼ teaspoon baking soda
1 tablespoon baking powder	¼ teaspoon ground nutmeg
1 teaspoon ground cinnamon	⅛ teaspoon ground ginger

In a large bowl, combine all ingredients. Spoon Pumpkin Bread Mix into a 1-pint glass jar. Attach a recipe card with the following instructions.

Pumpkin Bread

Pumpkin Bread Mix
1 cup canned pumpkin
½ cup apple juice concentrate

3 egg whites
⅓ cup plain nonfat yogurt
2 tablespoons honey

Preheat oven to 350 degrees. Spray 9x5x3-inch loaf pan with nonstick cooking spray. In a large mixing bowl, empty contents of Pumpkin Bread Mix. Add remaining ingredients. Pour batter into prepared loaf pan. Bake for 60 to 65 minutes or until toothpick inserted near middle comes out clean. Cool 10 minutes in pan before inverting onto a wire rack.

Oat Bran Muffin Mix

1 cup flour
1 tablespoon baking powder
½ teaspoon cinnamon
¼ cup packed brown sugar

¼ cup raisins
2¼ cups oat bran cereal
¼ cup chopped walnuts

Combine flour, baking powder, and cinnamon. Place in bottom of a glass jar. Continue layering ingredients in jar in order given. Attach a recipe card with the following instructions.

Oat Bran Muffins

1¼ cups skim milk
2 egg whites

2 tablespoons vegetable oil
Oat Bran Muffin Mix

Preheat oven to 350 degrees. In a large bowl, beat milk, egg whites, and oil with a spoon. Stir in Oat Bran Muffin Mix, and mix until well combined. Line muffin pans with paper baking cups, and fill cups ½ to ⅔ full. Bake for 25 to 30 minutes, testing with toothpick for doneness. Store in plastic bag and refrigerate.

Whole Wheat Cinnamon-Raisin Bread Mix
(low fat, low sugar)

3 cups whole wheat flour
2 teaspoons baking soda
¼ teaspoon salt

1½ teaspoons cinnamon
1 cup raisins
½ cup chopped pecans

In a large bowl, combine all ingredients. Spoon into a 1-quart glass jar, tapping down, if necessary. Attach a recipe card with the following instructions.

Whole Wheat Cinnamon-Raisin Bread

Whole Wheat Cinnamon-Raisin
Bread Mix

1½ cups low-fat plain yogurt
2 tablespoons honey

Preheat oven to 350 degrees. Spray two 7x4x3-inch loaf pans with nonstick cooking spray. In a large bowl, empty Whole Wheat Cinnamon-Raisin Bread Mix. Add yogurt and honey, mixing until well combined and fluffy. Pour into prepared loaf pans. Bake for 50 to 60 minutes or until loaves sound hollow when tapped. Invert to a wire rack to cool.

Honey-Whole Wheat Waffle Mix

(low fat, low sugar)

1¼ cups whole wheat flour
¾ cup all-purpose flour
1 teaspoon baking powder

½ teaspoon baking soda
½ teaspoon salt

In a large bowl, combine all ingredients. Spoon into a 1-pint widemouthed jar, tapping down if necessary. Attach a recipe card with the following instructions.

Honey–Whole Wheat Waffles

Honey–Whole Wheat Waffle Mix
4 teaspoons vegetable oil
3 tablespoons honey

3 egg whites
1½ cups low-fat vanilla yogurt

Preheat waffle iron. In a large bowl, empty Honey–Whole Wheat Waffle Mix. Add oil, honey, egg whites, and yogurt, stirring until moistened. Bake waffles in waffle iron according to manufacturers instructions. Serve with additional yogurt, if desired.

Heart-Healthy Carrot Cake Mix

½ cup chopped walnuts
2 cups whole wheat flour
1 tablespoon baking powder
½ teaspoon baking soda
1 teaspoon salt
1¼ teaspoons ground cinnamon

¼ teaspoon ground nutmeg
½ teaspoon ground ginger
⅛ teaspoon ground cloves
½ cup raisins
½ cup shredded coconut

Combine flour, baking powder, baking soda, salt, and spices. Place in bottom of a 1-quart glass jar. Layer remaining ingredients in order given. Attach a recipe card with the following instructions.

Heart-Healthy Carrot Cake

Heart-Healthy Carrot Cake Mix
2 eggs
¼ cup apple juice concentrate

1 cup skim or low-fat milk
2 cups grated carrots

Preheat oven to 400 degrees. Grease and lightly flour an 8-inch square cake pan. In a large bowl, empty Heart-Healthy Carrot Cake Mix, stirring to combine. Add eggs, apple juice concentrate, milk, and carrots. Beat with a spoon until well blended. Pour batter into prepared pan. Bake for 35 to 40 minutes or until toothpick inserted in center of cake comes out clean.

No Sugar Added
Tropical Island Cookie Mix

(sugar free, low fat)

1 cup quick-cooking oats
1 cup all-purpose flour
1 teaspoon baking powder
1 teaspoon baking soda
¼ teaspoon salt
¼ teaspoon nutmeg

½ cup oat or wheat bran
½ cup granulated sweetener
½ cup raisins
½ cup flaked coconut
½ cup chopped walnuts

In a 1-quart glass jar, layer ingredients in order given, combining flour, baking powder, baking soda, and salt. Attach a recipe card with the following instructions.

No Sugar Added Tropical Island Cookies

No Sugar Added Tropical Island
    Cookie Mix
2 large, very ripe bananas, mashed
¼ cup light banana-flavored yogurt

1 egg, slightly beaten
2 tablespoons vegetable oil
½ teaspoon vanilla

Preheat oven to 350 degrees. In a large bowl, empty No Sugar Added Tropical
Island Cookie Mix, stirring to combine. Add mashed bananas, yogurt, slightly
beaten egg, oil, and vanilla. Beat with spoon until well blended. Roll dough
into 1¼-inch balls, and place 2 inches apart on a lightly greased cookie sheet,
flattening cookie with back of a fork. Bake for 13 to 15 minutes or until just
beginning to brown. Immediately remove cookies to wire rack.

Applesauce-Spice Bar Mix
(low fat, low sugar)

¼ cup wheat bran
¼ cup sliced almonds
1 cup whole wheat flour
1 teaspoon baking powder

1½ teaspoons ground cinnamon
1 teaspoon ground ginger
¼ teaspoon ground nutmeg
¼ cup raisins

In a 1-pint widemouthed glass jar, layer ingredients in order given, combining flour, baking powder, and spices. Attach a recipe card with the following instructions.

Applesauce-Spice Bars

Applesauce-Spice Bar Mix
¼ cup egg substitute
2 tablespoons canola oil
½ cup fat-free plain yogurt

½ cup apple juice concentrate
1 teaspoon vanilla
1 cup unsweetened applesauce

Preheat oven to 350 degrees. Spray an 8-inch square baking pan with nonstick cooking spray. In a large bowl, empty contents of Applesauce-Spice Bar Mix, stirring to combine. Add egg substitute, oil, yogurt, juice, vanilla, and applesauce, beating with a spoon until well blended. Pour batter into prepared pan. Bake for 40 to 45 minutes or until toothpick inserted near center comes out clean. Cool in pan on wire rack. Cut into squares.

Fudgy Brownie Mix
(low fat)

1½ cups all-purpose flour
1 teaspoon baking powder
½ teaspoon baking soda

½ teaspoon salt
1¼ cups granulated sugar
¾ cup unsweetened cocoa powder

In a large bowl, combine all ingredients. Spoon into a 1-quart glass jar. Attach a recipe card with the following instructions.

Fudgy Brownies

1 (14 ounce) can fat-free sweetened,
    condensed milk
½ cup egg substitute

1 teaspoon vanilla
½ teaspoon butter flavoring

Preheat oven to 350 degrees. Spray a 9x13x2-inch baking pan with nonstick cooking spray. In a large bowl, combine condensed milk, egg substitute, vanilla, and butter flavoring, mixing well. Add Fudgy Brownie Mix, and stir until well combined. Pour into prepared baking pan, and bake for 18 to 22 minutes or until a toothpick inserted near center comes out clean. Cool in pan on wire rack.

For unto us a child is born,
unto us a son is given.

ISAIAH 9:6